D0817570

Help

Clarion Books
New York

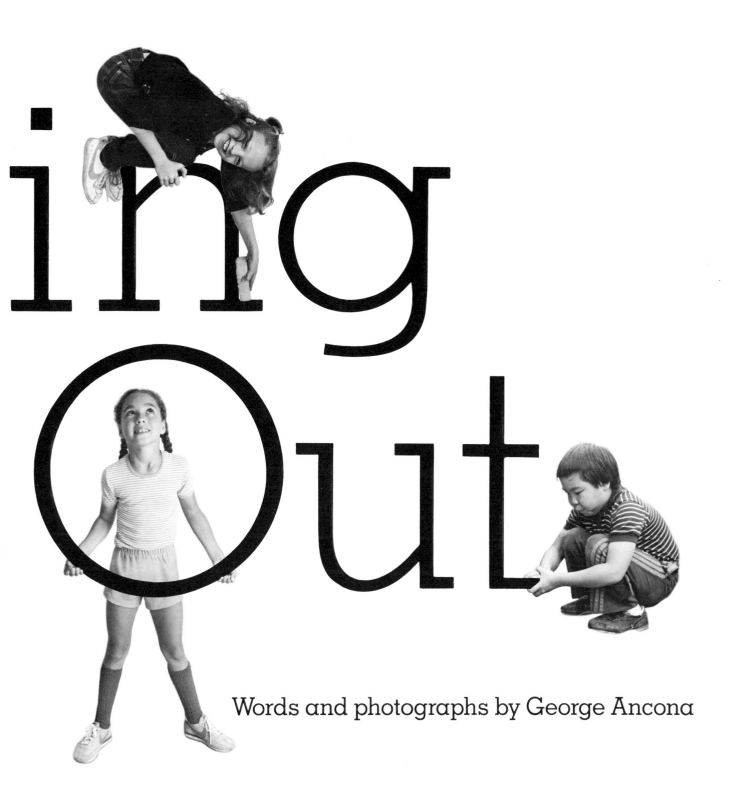

Words and photographs by George Ancona

To Marina

Clarion Books
a Houghton Mifflin Company imprint
215 Park Avenue South, New York, NY 10003
Copyright © 1985 by George Ancona

For information about permission to reproduce
selections from this book, write to Permissions,
Houghton Mifflin Company, 2 Park Street, Boston, MA 02108
Printed in the USA

Library of Congress Cataloging-in-Publication Data
Ancona, George.
  Helping out.

  Summary: Explores in black-and-white photographs the
special relationship between adults and children
working together in many different settings.
  1. Helping behavior—Juvenile literature.   2. Children
and adults—Juvenile literature. [1. Helpfulness—
Pictorial works] I. Title.
BF637.H4A53 1985   158'.24   84-14995
ISBN 0-89919-278-5   PA ISBN 0-395-54774-1

BP 10 9 8 7 6 5 4

Some of the best times of my life were spent as a little boy helping out a grown-up. Sometimes I would work with my mother or father. At other times, it was a neighbor or relative.

One neighbor was an auto mechanic. After school I would go to his garage and sweep up. For this, he would pay me the money I needed to go to the movies on Saturday.

When I was older, I spent one summer helping my godfather dig a cellar for his new house.

All the time I was sweeping, digging, or carrying, I was watching and learning. I was also having a great time being in the adult world.

I decided to make this book after seeing what some young people do to help others. Perhaps you can think of more ways that *you* can help those around you.

Helping out can be as simple as being there to hand someone a tool when he needs it.

In early spring, you can help to plant seeds in the vegetable garden. Soon they will sprout and grow into many good things to eat.

You can turn some chores into fun, like washing the car on a hot summer's day.

Helping rake the fall
leaves is a chore that
tells you winter is on
its way.

And everyone welcomes
help digging out after
a snowfall.

You can spend a cozy winter afternoon in grandpa's workshop helping to sort out all those mixed-up nails, screws, nuts, and bolts.

On a farm, one of your chores may be shooing chickens and then gently gathering their warm eggs.

Out on the hot sunny fields, the farmer needs helping hands to cut, bale, and stack the hay, which will feed the cows next winter.

Using a shepherd's crook, the rancher's son catches sheep by their legs. Now his dad can examine them before sending them to market.

On a dude ranch,
there are always horses
to help saddle for the
guests to ride.

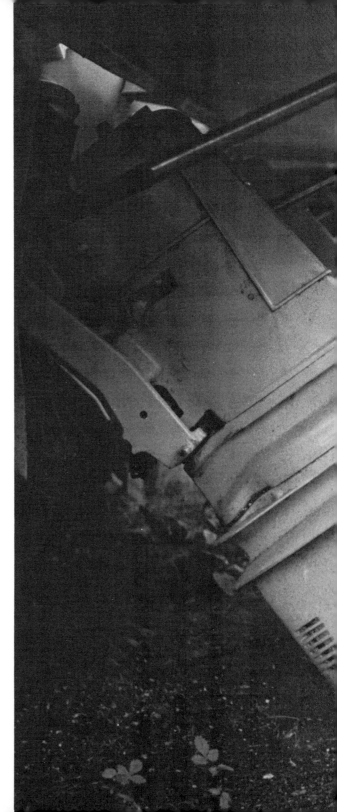

When you own a boat,
you must scrape the
barnacles off the bottom
before putting it back
in the saltwater.

No matter where you
live, the kitchen, with its
warm, good smells,
is a great place to help.
Except for slicing an
onion, which makes
you cry.

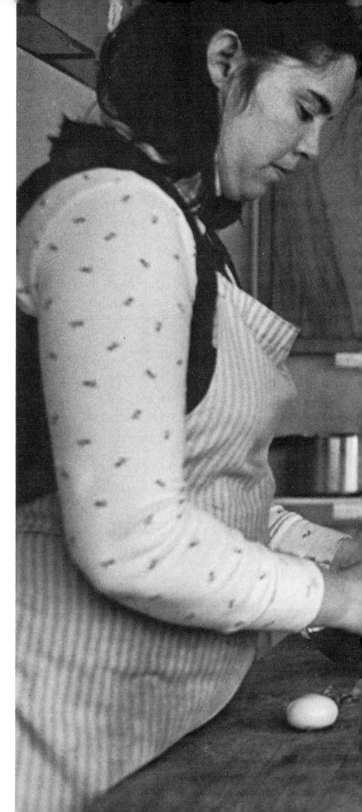

Feeding the baby can
be a funny, yucky job.

Some jobs can be dirty,
like changing the oil
in the engine of a car.

At school, a teacher needs help keeping the classroom neat and clean.

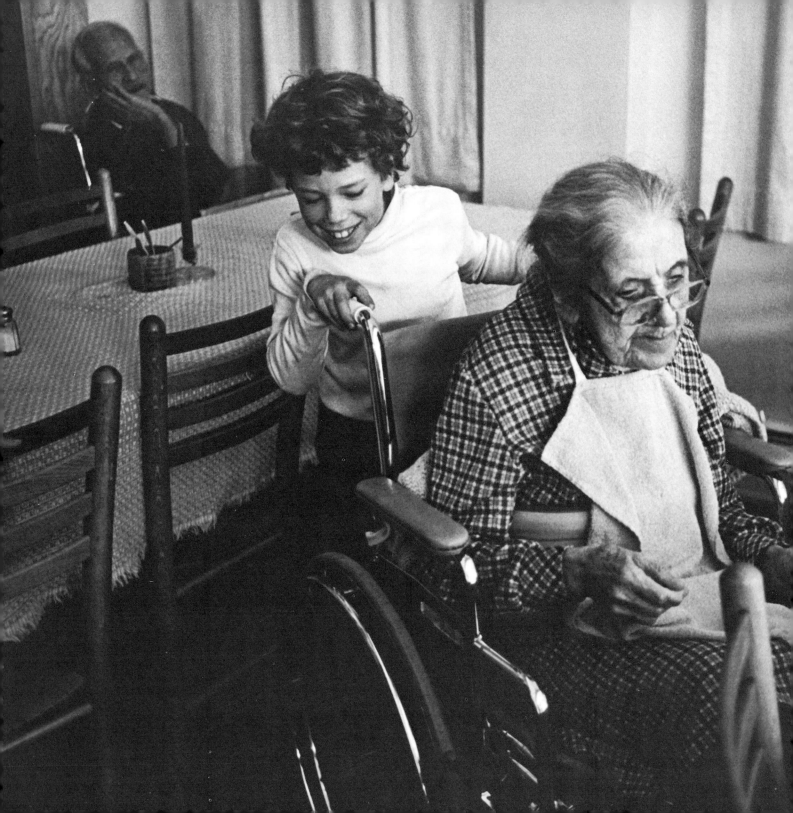

Helping out also means
doing something for
those who cannot do it
for themselves.

Teenagers can become volunteers in a hospital where they help nurses. Because of their uniforms, they are called candy stripers.

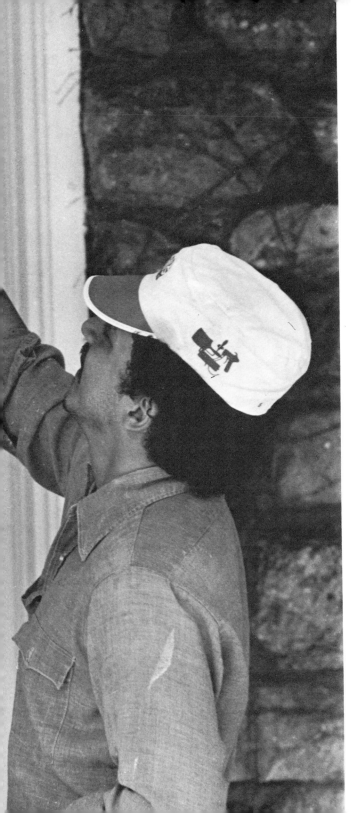

When you work
alongside an adult
and do a good job,
you feel pretty big.

By letting a young person help, a grown-up shares his or her skills. This girl's dad is a glassblower. She is helping him make a perfume bottle.

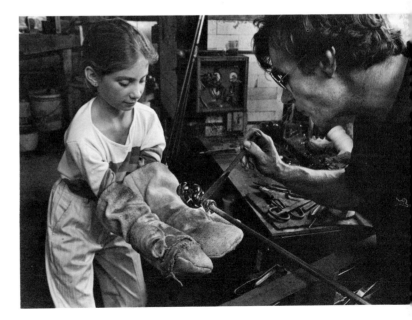

After you learn to do things well, you can begin to get paid for your work.

But the best thing about helping out is that it can bring two people closer together.

I would like to thank the people who allowed
me to photograph what they do: in particular,
the folks at the Threefold Foundation;
the Green Meadow Waldorf School; and
Nyack Hospital and
the Duryea family.
Thanks also to
J. P. Metcalf,
Tammy Francois,
the Jean-Jacques family,
the Woodcock family,
the Turner family,
the Serrano family,
the Bosch family,
the Kolstein family,
the Sutherland family,
the Yamamoto family,
the Conti family,
the Booth family,
Dr. Paul Scharff,
the Thompson family,
the Hochhausen/Boersma family,
Corina Mann, and
Gina, Helga, and Pablo Ancona
for helping out.